THE LOST HOUSE OF LOCKWOOD LAKE

Written by Sana Rasoul
Illustrated by Dan Whisker

hachette
LEARNING

ISBN: 9781036000608

Text © Sana Rasoul
Design, illustrations and layout © 2025 Hodder & Stoughton Limited
First published in 2025 by Hachette Learning,
An Hachette UK Company
Carmelite House, 50 Victoria Embankment, London EC4Y 0DZ

www.HachetteLearning.com
The authorised representative in the EEA is Hachette Ireland, 8 Castlecourt Centre, Dublin 15, D15 XTP3, Ireland (email: info@hbgi.ie)

Impression number 10 9 8 7 6 5 4 3 2 1
Year 2029 2028 2027 2026 2025

Author: Sana Rasoul
Illustrator: Dan Whisker/The Bright Agency
Series Editor: Catherine Coe
Educational Consultant: Pauline Allen
Page layout: Rocket Design (East Anglia) Ltd

With thanks to the schools that took part in the development of *Reading Planet Cosmos*, including: Ancaster CE Primary School, Ancaster; Downsway Primary School, Reading; Ferry Lane Primary School, London; Foxborough Primary School, Slough; Griffin Park Primary School, Blackburn; St Barnabas CE First & Middle School, Pershore; Tranmoor Primary School, Doncaster; and Wilton CE Primary School, Wilton.

The Publishers would like to thank the following for permission to reproduce copyright material. Design: © tutti frutti/stock.adobe.com; © thongchainak/stock.adobe.com; © frilled dragon/stock.adobe.com

All rights reserved. Apart from any use permitted under UK copyright law, no part of this publication may be reproduced or transmitted in any form or by any means, electronic or mechanical, including photocopying and recording, or held within any information storage and retrieval system, without permission in writing from the publisher or under licence from the Copyright Licensing Agency Limited. Further details of such licences (for reprographic reproduction) may be obtained from the Copyright Licensing Agency Limited, www.cla.co.uk

A catalogue record for this title is available from the British Library.

Printed in the UK

Hachette UK's policy is to use papers that are natural, renewable and recyclable products and made from wood grown in sustainable forests and other controlled sources. The logging and manufacturing processes are expected to conform to the environmental regulations of the country of origin.

To order please visit www.HachetteLearning.com or contact Customer Service at education@hachette.co.uk / +44 (0)1235 827827

Contents

1 Adventurers United 4

2 The Wail 16

3 The Wizard's Tools 29

4 The Secret Doorway 34

5 An Unexpected Key 39

6 The Cage 44

7 The Four Elements 50

8 The Number One Rule
   of Alchemy 58

Adventurers United

"Are you sure your parents won't find out?" Peter asked.

He pushed his glasses back on his nose and turned to face Karim. They were sitting on the floor, in Karim's bedroom, like they did every Friday after school. A trail of sweet wrappers, comic books and a half-eaten pizza surrounded them.

"They won't be able to see the lake properly, not from here. Besides, they always go to the supermarket on Saturday mornings, so it'll just be Nan in the house tomorrow," Karim said.

Peter ran his hand through his hair, the colour of burnt oranges, and shoved a sourball in his mouth. He twisted his face and spat it out.

"Why didn't you say so earlier? I was getting nervous for no reason."

"Why are you nervous? It was your idea to go swimming in the lake, remember?" Karim said.

When Peter didn't respond, Karim got to his feet and walked over to the window by his bed.

In the distance, he could make out the shimmering glow of the lake. Sometimes, it would shine bright, like a torch aimed at his window. Other times, the colour reminded Karim of a dying leaf. Peter joined him by the window, and for a few seconds neither of them spoke a word, as though hypnotised by the alluring colours of Lockwood Lake.

"Are you having second thoughts? We don't have to go if you don't want to." Karim turned to Peter.

"No way!" Peter replied. "I just want to make sure we don't get caught. Mum and Dad would ground me forever if they found out I was anywhere near the lake. Mum said it's deeper than it looks, and it can get actual waves, just like the ocean."

"Yeah, my parents don't like me going there either," moaned Karim. "Dad hasn't taken me to the lake since the whole fishing-rod drama."

"What happened to his fishing rod?" Peter asked.

"It kept snapping off beneath the water," Karim said, remembering how annoyed Dad had been.

"What if the stories are true ..." Peter gave Karim a knowing look.

"Which one exactly?" Karim chuckled. "There's so many about the lake, I can't keep up."

"You know which one I'm talking about! The lost house under the lake," a serious-looking Peter replied.

Karim had grown up in Cemetery Grove, so he'd heard his fair share of creepy stories about some of the houses around town. None captivated him more than the mystery of the lost house at Lockwood Lake.

There were many versions of the tale, but they all began the same way, with a storm that tore through Cemetery Grove. The storm destroyed most of the buildings, except one.

A towering house had been lost for good after it mysteriously sank to the bottom of the lake, never to resurface.

No one ever dared go in the lake, believing it to be cursed. Things always seemed to disappear in the water, including the owner of the lost house. It was part of the reason why Karim had agreed to go swimming with Peter in the first place, even though he was forbidden to do so by his parents. He was utterly intrigued about where the lost house had gone.

Of course, Karim didn't expect to see an actual house down there, but he might find a treasure or two that he could add to his collectables. He had a small treasure chest that Nan had given him for his birthday, which he filled with items he thought were interesting or valuable.

"Do you think the lake water glows like that because of the algae?" Karim asked, still looking out of the window. "That's what our science teacher told me."

"Or maybe it's the lights being turned on in the lost house," Peter said mysteriously.

"That would be pretty cool!" Karim admitted.

"Do you have everything ready for tomorrow?" Peter dug into his pocket and pulled out a scrunched-up piece of paper.

"Not that list again!" Karim rolled his eyes – every time they prepared for an adventure, Peter always wrote down a list of things they needed and forced Karim to listen to it over and over again.

"It's important to be prepared," Peter said, reading his mind. "Goggles," he began reading from the list.

"Check," Karim said.

"Wetsuits."

"Check."

"And finally, a bag in case we find anything good," Peter finished off.

"Check."

Peter smiled and put the paper back into his pocket.

"Shall we seal our mission with a handshake?" Peter asked, giving Karim a pointed look.

Karim stretched out his hand and they performed their secret handshake, which meant there was no turning back now.

"To Adventurers United!" they shouted at the same time. Karim and Peter had founded the secret organisation for explorers and collectors during the summer. So far, they were its only members, but they had successfully carried out six explorations in Cemetery Grove. Karim could never forget the time they both climbed the tall, twisted oak tree near the 'Ghost House'.

The next morning, Karim woke up to the sound of wheels squeaking against the wooden floor just outside his bedroom. He crawled out of bed and opened the door to find Mum dragging a small suitcase past him.

"Are you heading out already?" Karim tried to curb the excitement in his voice, but it was hard to contain. He wanted to jump up and down and wiggle his hands in the air just so he could release all the adrenaline pumping through him.

"Yes, sorry, darling. I did want to have breakfast with you, but your dad and I have a lot to be getting on with. Nan's been awake for a while, so she'll probably have her nap in a bit."

"What's in the suitcase?" Karim asked.

"Clothes for the charity shop," Mum replied. "What will you get up to whilst we're out?"

"I'll probably invite Peter round."

Mum smiled. "You two are inseparable! Dad and I will do the weekly grocery shop as well, so we won't be back for a while. You'll look after Nan if she needs anything, won't you?"

"Sure," Karim said.

Mum gave him a light kiss on the forehead and not long after, Karim heard the front door close and the car engine grumbling. He looked out of the window – the sky was a clear blue and there was hardly any wind. It was the perfect morning for a swim. The lake looked eerily calm too, like it hadn't yet woken up from its slumber.

Karim headed downstairs for some breakfast.

Nan was sitting in her favourite armchair, with a cup of tea in her hand.

"Peter's going to come round in a bit," Karim told her. "We're going to play out in the garden."

"How lovely. I'm afraid I won't be much company. I've got a bit of a headache."

"Why don't you go and lie down for a bit," Karim suggested. Normally he liked spending time with his nan but he had other arrangements that morning. More exciting ones.

"You read my mind! I was just about to do that," Nan said.

Karim grabbed a slice of bread and kept Nan company until she finished her tea. Not long after she'd gone up to her room to sleep, the doorbell rang.

When Karim opened the door, Peter was there, puffing as if he'd been running.

"What is in there?" Karim pointed to the bulky bag hanging over Peter's shoulder. It was nearly as big as he was. "Why have you got so much stuff with you? I don't remember the list being that long."

"I added a few things we might need, like snacks and drinks," Peter explained.

"We've got to be quick. Nan usually sleeps for at least an hour, but if she wakes up and finds we're not in the garden, we'll be in trouble."

Karim and Peter followed the dirt track that weaved down to the lake.

As they walked side by side, Karim found it difficult to concentrate on what Peter was saying. Something about the different types of fish that lived in lakes. The closer they got to their destination, the more nervous Karim began to feel, which was weird, because he hardly ever got nervous before an Adventurers United mission.

He dragged his feet past ferns and reeds and bulrushes until finally they stopped in front of the lake. From the window in his bedroom, the lake always looked miniscule, but it was a different beast when he stood so close to it.

It had been a while since Karim had been down here – months even. The water was a mossy colour today, with floating plants and fallen logs drifting on the surface. A ripple in the water caught Karim's attention, and he leaned forward to get a closer look.

"Over there!" Karim pointed to an orange-beaked swan. It looked up at him with a bored expression on its face, then proceeded to dip its head in the water.

"You're not scared, are you?" Peter teased. "Swans are defensive by nature – if you disturb their nest, they might come for you." He sniggered.

There were many reasons why Peter was Karim's best friend, and one of them was the fact that Peter was a walking encyclopaedia and Karim felt smarter just by being around him.

"I'm not scared. I've just never seen one so close up before." Karim put on his goggles and slung a small bag over his shoulders. He was hoping to find a buried coin or a cryptic message in a glass bottle somewhere in the lake – the possibilities really were endless.

Next to him, Peter folded his clothes away neatly, then put the goggles over his eyes.

"What if we see the lost house down there? What do you think it looks like?" Peter's eyes glittered with excitement.

Karim laughed, startling the swan who quickly swam in the opposite direction.

"I know you're really excited, but don't get your hopes up. Even if the stories are true, and there is a house underneath the water, it would be right at the bottom, and we won't be able to hold our breaths long enough to see it. You said yourself – the lake is deep."

Karim liked to imagine there was a fully intact house below them, rooms packed with old maps and other treasures, but it was hard to believe.

That didn't stop Peter from having a dreamy gaze though, his eyes seeming bigger and brighter than they actually were. Yet, it was Karim who braved the water first. He dipped his toe in hesitantly and was pleasantly surprised to find it lukewarm.

"Get in!" he called Peter over. "How long can you hold your breath for?"

"I can only do thirty seconds, but free divers can hold their breath for much longer," Peter said.

They were floating in the water as a tiny ray of sun broke through the clouds. Karim felt a small sense of satisfaction at their rebellious act. He couldn't wait to tell everyone at school that they'd braved the mysterious Lockwood Lake. They'd be legends! Everyone would want to know what they'd found.

"That's pretty decent – there's no way I could hold my breath for that long!" Karim said.

"Are you ready to see what we can find?" Peter said, not waiting for Karim to respond. He disappeared beneath the water and, not wanting to be left behind, Karim gulped as much air as possible before diving headfirst into the lake.

Peter was busy flicking away the floating seaweed surrounding him. Karim swam next to him, and they began searching the lake. The pressure of the water was harder to push through the deeper they swam.

When he became short of breath, Karim signalled for Peter to swim back up to the surface.

"I couldn't see the bottom of the lake, and the water isn't very clear, is it?" Karim complained after he caught his breath.

"Let's try to dive a bit deeper," Peter said.

Karim was glad that he had been forced to take swimming lessons every Saturday since he was six. He pinched his nose, preparing to go back down. He was a strong swimmer, and so was Peter, but they weren't under the water long before Karim felt like an invisible hand pulling him down.

Panicking, he turned to Peter, who seemed to be sinking into the darkness below. Kicking his legs behind him as hard as he could, Karim grabbed onto Peter's hand, desperately trying to pull both of them up. But Peter was too heavy and the current too strong to resist, as it hurled them into the depths of Lockwood Lake.

The Wail

As they were pulled deeper into the water, a desperate Karim used his dwindling energy to move closer to Peter. He knew he'd run out of air soon.

Peter reached for Karim's hand as they passed a dazzling display of green light. It looked like fireworks had erupted in the lake, and for a split-second Karim hoped it was someone coming down to rescue them.

Then, the strangest thing happened: Karim felt his entire body relax. The tightness in his chest was gone, and his lungs no longer felt like they were screaming for air.

Stunned, Karim realised he could breathe through his nose without choking, as if he wasn't under the water at all. Peter stared at him with a confused expression – even behind the goggles Karim could see Peter's eyes widen in disbelief. He pointed to his mouth and nose and Karim nodded in response.

The heavy current seemed to have vanished, like their need for air. There was only a still coldness as the temperature dipped around them.

They floated on the spot for a few minutes, trying to make sense of the impossible. How were they breathing underwater? Peter raised his hand and they high-fived each other. No longer deterred by the lack of oxygen, they swam further down. Karim kept his eyes peeled for sparkling treasures, but Peter seemed to be on another mission entirely as he raced to the bottom of the lake.

Karim knew what Peter was looking for: the lost house. He was just about to join Peter when his attention was diverted by the sound of splashing water above his head.

Karim had been so caught up in the magical tales of the lost house that he hadn't considered the possibility that something else could be in the lake with them. The next splash of water sent a chilling ripple up his spine. By now, Peter was a shadowy blur below him.

Suddenly, a loud wail shook the lake from top to bottom. Karim covered his ears with his hands, and in the corner of his eye, he saw a flash of green.

From the murky water, a pair of egg-white eyes peered down at him. Then, a spindly figure emerged from the whirlpool. Karim tried to scream, but no noise escaped his lips. They remained shut, paralysed by fear. Even his body seemed to be on pause mode. Grabbing Karim by the arm, Peter pointed below them and they dived deeper down into the lake.

Karim was unable to drag his eyes away from the creature with long inky black hair, sharp canine teeth and green-tinged skin. It opened its mouth and let out another ear-splitting wail.

The creature stared Karim in the eyes before reaching out a bony arm towards him. As it slithered in the water, closing in on him, Karim turned round and began swimming frantically into the depths of Lockwood Lake. He knew Peter was swimming next to him but all Karim could hear was the beating of his heart. It drowned out his fear for a moment, until he felt the creature's cold skin brush against his leg. It was trying to wrap its fingers around his ankle, wailing and wailing until Karim felt like his ears were going to burst from his head.

That was when Peter stopped, abruptly and without warning. He was staring at the silhouette of a slender, cylindrical building. It jutted out of the lakebed, like a lighthouse, made of stone. Pondweed covered the exterior of the house. It was many storeys high and it looked oddly familiar to Karim, even though he was sure he hadn't seen it before.

Karim turned to Peter who had his mouth open. Could it really be ... the lost house?

Miraculously, the creature was no longer following them, so Karim and Peter made their way to the house. As they got closer, the door flew open and a man with grey hair poked his head out of the door. He had a beard that curled around his face and a moustache that flicked up at both ends. The man did not have any goggles or breathing equipment on. He stared at Karim and Peter, and then pointed behind them. Karim turned and saw the creature a few metres away.

If Karim had been able to scream, he would have.

"Get in here! Quick!" came the man's frantic voice, and to Karim's surprise he could hear him as clearly as if they were on dry land.

They bolted towards the house.

"Quickly now! Shut the door behind you. Come on!" the man yelled as the banshee's wails grew louder. It felt like the entire lake was crying out in anguish.

Karim shut the door behind him and ran to the furthest corner of the room as the man put a hand to his lips. The man looked out of the window and after a few minutes had passed he turned to Karim and Peter.

"It's gone," the man said.

"We c-can talk?" Peter stammered.

"I can hear you!" a stunned Karim said, looking round him. "How come there isn't any water in here?"

"Powerful magic ..." the man replied, and there was deep longing in his voice.

"Who are you?" Peter asked the man. "Is this the house that survived the storm? It is, isn't it? Did you swim down here too? Is that how you found it? How do we get back up?"

"Let him talk!" Karim nudged Peter.

Almost instantly, the man's demeanour changed. He grinned at them, but it wasn't a pleasant smile. The man's teeth were crooked and yellow, and there was something unsettling in his eyes. He turned his back to them, grabbed a cloak from the hook by the door and paused.

"I gave up on the idea of anyone venturing this far down the lake a long time ago."

"What do you mean? What's going on? Who are you?" It was Karim's turn to hurl questions at the man.

"Please, tell us what's happening! How do we get back up to the surface?" Peter cried.

The man laughed.

"Oh, you can't go back up, I'm afraid. You see, now that you've entered the house, you can no longer leave."

"W-what?" Peter stuttered.

"I used my magic to save this house, and myself, when the storm came a century ago. The rest of the town crumbled, and the Council of Wizards found out. Since I used magic for personal gain, they tied me to this house ... to this lake ... for eternity."

Karim wracked his brain, drawing together all the conversations he had heard about the storm over the years. It felt like he was rearranging a complicated jigsaw puzzle until they fit neatly into place.

In one version of the story, a powerful wizard lived in Cemetery Grove, but he'd disappeared right after the storm.

"You ... you're the wizard in the stories!" Karim yelled.

The wizard bowed.

"I thought my luck had ran out, but here you both are. Turns out, I don't need that banshee after all."

"Banshee?" Peter repeated. "That's what that creature was?"

The wizard nodded.

"The Council were smart; this wretched curse they've had me under could only be broken by another human, not a creature of the lake. I've wasted so much time ..."

Karim was more and more confused.

"What curse?"

"Take good care of my home," the Wizard said. "I can't take any of my magic or possessions with me, but it's a price I'm willing to pay." He stared around him, as though memorising every inch of the place.

"You're leaving?" Peter asked, a nervous edge to his voice.

"You can't abandon us here!" Karim said.

"Oh, but I can." The wizard narrowed his eyes. "I've waited for this moment for over a century."

Karim gasped. A century?

"Well, I'd love to stay and chat some more, but I'm desperate to see the sky again," the wizard jeered and opened the door. The water remained outside, as if an invisible barrier was protecting the house from being engulfed.

Karim ran after the wizard, but as soon as he placed one foot out of the house, a blast of water pushed him back inside and the door slammed shut in his face.

Peter ran forwards, twisting the doorknob and trying to leave the house, but the same thing happened to him.

"Ouch!" Peter cried, hobbling to his feet.

Karim ran to the window, trying to get it open, but it had no latch or handle. He banged on the glass as hard as he could.

"Please! Don't leave us here! We want to go home!" Karim screamed and Peter joined him, both screaming and banging their fists on the glass until the wizard turned to them. His face was full of malice. The wizard said nothing, only cackling before disappearing into the distance.

Karim and Peter were left on their own.

"What are we going to do?" a desperate Karim asked, but it was the first time in a long while that Peter was lost for words. Karim was used to hearing him blurt out all sorts of solutions, backed up with facts and statistics.

"There must be a way out." Karim tried the door again but with each pull, the door flew open and shut again. The wizard was right – they couldn't leave!

"The window," Peter said quietly. "Maybe it's just the door that won't let us pass. Let's break the glass and go out that way."

Picking up a bulky ornament from the table, Peter walked over to the window, but Karim grabbed the vase from him and put it back down.

"No, we can't do that. The banshee will be able to come in then, and who knows what else!"

Peter's face fell.

"Even if we find a way to get out there," Karim started, "how are we supposed to swim all the way up? What if we get captured by the banshee?"

"You're right," Peter said quietly, looking around him. "Our best chance is to search the house. There must be something here that can help us figure out what to do next."

Karim was thinking about how worried his parents must be by now. They didn't even know he'd gone to the lake with Peter. He'd lied to Nan as well, and now he was paying the price. Karim wondered if this was what his dad meant when he said nothing in life is free. That there was always a price to pay. Karim had learned a valuable lesson: lies are expensive.

"Do you think our parents will find us?" Karim asked.

Peter's eyes lit up.

"Of course! We left our clothes and my bag by the lake. They'll see them and get a search and rescue team down here." A little colour returned to Peter's cheeks as he spoke.

"Unless the wizard took all of our stuff so no one would suspect we were at the lake," Karim said.

A shocked squeal came out of Peter's lips. Karim felt bad for crushing his hopes, but even if their parents looked for them in the lake, would they search this far down?

"Okay, let's think about this," Peter said. "So far, we know that we can't leave the house because of the curse. The only way out is if –"

"If what?" Karim asked.

"If we trap someone in the house, like the wizard did to us. We have to wait until someone else comes down here."

"Peter! We can't! That would be a horrible thing to do!"

"I know it's bad ... but what other choice do we have?"

"You heard what the wizard said – no one comes down this far. We should never have done that," Karim said.

"I'm sorry, I didn't mean that really. I'm just really scared," Peter admitted.

"Me too, but we'll find a way. We have to – now let's start by searching the house."

They walked up a set of steps made of stone, just like the outside of the house. Karim tried not to look down. He took his goggles off, but Peter kept his on so he could see properly.

If someone had told him earlier that morning that he would find himself stuck, at the bottom of Lockwood Lake, in a house he didn't actually think existed, he'd have laughed. But laughing was the last thing Karim felt like doing.

The house would have been shrouded in darkness if it weren't for the bioluminescent plants that decorated the rooms. The boys started at the top floor – which only had one room on it. Peter opened the door to a tiny room, with a circular window facing the back of the house. Outside the house, it was eerily quiet and grey.

"What time do you think it is?" Karim asked Peter, but Peter was too fascinated by the room to respond.

A jellyfish chandelier hung from the ceiling and there was a telescope positioned next to the window. Karim imagined the wizard up here, all those years, plotting and scheming his way out.

Peter frowned.

"Didn't the wizard say something about the banshee?"

"Yes, he did," Karim remembered. "Something about not needing the banshee any more. Do you think the wizard was trying to capture the banshee so he could escape the house?"

"But it didn't work because the banshee already lives in the lake," Peter added.

"But if the wizard has been down here for so long, he must have been working on another plan," Peter suggested. "Let's look in the other rooms for a way out. There's nothing here besides that telescope."

Peter walked out of the room, but Karim lingered for a while.

He felt compelled to look into the telescope. Did the wizard use the telescope to keep track of the banshee? Karim fiddled with the lens until he got a clear view of the lake, and of something else. Egg-white eyes, and a shadow floating back and forth. It paused outside the window and ran one long black fingernail down the glass as it began to scream. Karim ran out of the room so fast he nearly slipped trying to make it down the stairs.

"Peter! Peter!" he shouted.

Standing at the foot of the stairs on the floor below, Peter turned to him.

"What is it?" he asked.

"B-banshee," Karim stammered, pointing above him.

The Wizard's Tools

"Where's the banshee? In the house?" a frantic Peter yelled, his eyes darting back and forth.

"No, I saw one by the window in the room upstairs." Karim shivered.

"It can't get in, can it?" Peter asked.

"I don't think so ... but let's stay away from the windows in case it spots us again," Karim said quietly.

They stayed on the same floor, entering a room half the size of Karim's at home, but containing twice as much stuff. There were glowing orbs floating in mid-air and a large map that covered the wall on one side of the room. The map did not look like any Karim had seen before, or at least, not of a world that Karim was aware existed. The places marked on the map had unusual sounding names like 'Petterflee' and 'Juicemoon'.

In the corner of the room, there were empty vials neatly lined upon the shelf, and a huge grey cauldron with what looked like a large wooden spoon inside it. On the other side of the cauldron, there were jars filled with all kinds of plants and herbs. Karim had never seen a rainbow-coloured plant before, and it reminded him of sparkling confetti. The jar was labelled 'bunglesead'.

"Wow!" Karim said, not believing his eyes.

Karim walked over to the cauldron and looked inside. It smelled of flowers and grass. Next to that was a large gold leather-bound book. It looked ancient, smelled musty and was heavy to carry. *The Perfect Guide to the Perfect Mix* read the title on the cover. Karim sat on the floor and began reading.

The pages were filled with recipes, just like a cookbook, with measurements and careful instructions. For a fraction of a second, Karim almost forgot that he was stuck under Lockwood Lake.

"What have you got there?" Peter asked.

"It looks like a potion book," Karim said, sliding the book across to Peter, who flipped through the pages.

"Have you seen this one here?" Peter laughed. "It's a potion to stop sneezing forever."

༄ Potion to Eliminate Sneezing ༄

- Mix one-part Humming Lotus with two-parts Black Sea Salt.
- Stir in the juice of prunes with one cup of saliva.
- Once the potion is thick and clumpy and has turned brown, drink immediately.

Karim pulled a face.

"Yuck! That does not sound tasty."

"It would take so long to fill a whole cup with saliva!" Peter laughed, and Karim laughed harder.

"This one sounds worse!" Karim showed Peter the 'Potion to Extract Ear Wax'.

❧ Potion to Extract Ear Wax ☙

- 1 teaspoon of wart juice
- 3 bunglesead leaves
- 2 dried worms
- Once the potion turns a light pink, pour into both earholes. The wax will then leak out of your ears.

"I feel sick." Peter clutched his tummy and pretended to throw up.

A distant howl in the background brought Karim back to reality, and he had a sudden realisation.

"Hey, Peter, have you felt hungry or thirsty since we got into the lake?"

"Now that I think about it, I don't think I have ... and you know how much I love to eat."

"What is happening to us?" Karim said.

"I don't know ..." Peter screwed up his face. "I should never have made us come down here. I'm sorry."

"You didn't make me do anything. I wanted to come, remember?" Trying to sound upbeat, Karim put an arm around Peter but his friend still looked deflated, like a balloon had popped inside of him.

"Come on, let's keep searching the house. Maybe we'll get lucky and find a clue or spell to get us out. I don't think it'll be in this book." Karim put *The Perfect Guide to the Perfect Mix* back where he found it and when he turned round, Peter was half hidden behind a small cupboard.

"What's in there?" Karim asked.

A faint white light was coming out of the cupboard, which made Peter look ghostly white. Peter turned around and showed Karim a small crystal ball, with swirling white clouds inside it. When Karim reached out to touch the glass, it felt icy-cold against his skin and a tingling sensation shot up his arm.

"Woah!" he said, pulling his hand away.

"Crystal balls are supposed to show you something ..." a hopeful Peter said, peering into the glass.

The room fell quiet, and Karim didn't realise he was holding his breath until he let it out.

"Can you see anything?" Karim asked Peter.

Peter shook his head.

"You try – maybe I'm missing something."

Karim took the crystal ball from Peter and looked inside. The swirling clouds continued to move around the glass, reminding him of a grey storm.

"Nope, nothing," Karim sighed.

"Oh well, it was worth a try," Peter said, putting the crystal ball back into the cupboard.

"I've got goosebumps everywhere," Karim whispered.

"Yeah, same, but it's probably from how cold the crystal ball is," Peter reasoned.

Karim yawned. "I'm getting tired."

"Me too," Peter admitted.

"What do you think the time is up there?" Karim tried to swallow his sadness.

Peter said nothing and Karim understood. It was too painful to think about how they were so far away.

Karim and Peter entered another room with a large four-poster bed and a sofa. A tapestry of mythical creatures and celestial landscapes adorned the walls. Empty glass bottles were on the small table beside the bed, which was stacked with plush purple cushions.

Karim lay flat on the bed, hoping it would ease the pounding in his head. Peter lay on the sofa and before Karim knew it, the soft, rhythmic hum of waves lulled them into sleep.

Unbeknown to either of them, a shadow lurked outside the window. Every now and then, its face appeared behind the glass. The banshee's hair was entangled with seaweed, its hungry eyes sweeping the room.

The Secret Doorway

Karim's dreams were filled with dancing fish and coral reefs, but as soon as he woke and opened his eyes, he was faced with the unsettling reality of being trapped in the lost house. Forever, if he didn't find a way out. Confused and disorientated, Karim threw the covers to the side and got out of bed. Opposite him, Peter was curled up on the sofa.

Karim stumbled to the corner of the room and stared into the cracked mirror hanging on the wall. He had huge bags under his eyes, and his hair was a tangled brown mess. He put a hand through it and caught a shadow in the reflection of the glass. Karim snapped his head round, and in the window behind him he saw a ghostly figure. Long, flowing hair swirled in the water. Like snakes, wriggling towards their prey. The banshee was outside, its eyes glowing with rage as Karim scrambled across the room.

"Get up, Peter! Get up!" Karim shouted but Peter flicked his hands away.

"Get up!" Karim tried again until Peter finally opened his eyes.

"What? Let me sleep a little longer ..." Peter groaned.

The house seemed to react to the banshee's angry wails, pulsating with energy.

Peter was wide awake now. He stood up and stared out of the window.

"Let's get out of this room!" Karim pulled a stunned Peter to the door. They moved from room to room, but the banshee seemed to follow them each time. It gave Karim the creeps. He just wanted to get away from its watchful eyes.

On the ground floor, they found a place hidden behind a curtain made out of kelp. They stepped inside and discovered a small closet that had no clothes or shoes or hangers – and no windows. The wails of the banshee eventually stopped.

Karim breathed a sigh of relief but Peter – who was cowering in the corner – looked like he might pass out from fear.

"I think it's gone," Karim said, but it took another couple of minutes for Peter's rigid shoulders to relax.

"The banshee can't find a way in, can it?" Peter asked.

"I don't think so – the wizard said that the curse couldn't be broken with sea creatures which probably means they can't get in the house at all."

Peter breathed a sigh of relief.

"It's not stopped the banshee from trying though, has it?" Peter remarked, but Karim was only half-listening.

"What's that behind your shoulder?" Karim could see the gleam of a shiny metal lock.

Without looking behind him, Peter screamed and wriggled away.

"What is it? What did you see?" Peter yelled. "Is anything on me?"

"Calm down! It's only a latch," Karim said, pushing a small wooden table aside to reveal a hidden door. It looked like a secret doorway.

Karim and Peter looked at each other, and for the first time since they entered the house, Karim felt a burst of positivity course through his veins. This could be a way out!

"It's locked," Peter said, rattling the heavy lock.

Karim looked around the room for a tool he could use to unlock it, but the room was bare and he had no idea how to pick locks anyway.

"Can you hear that noise?" Peter said.

"What noise?" Karim asked.

"Shh ... listen," Peter put a hand to his lips, just like the wizard had done when the banshee was prowling outside the house.

Eventually, Karim heard a soft hum. It drifted into his ears, like a song sung from very far away.

"I can hear it!" Karim said.

"I think it's coming from behind the door." Peter pressed his ear against the frame of the door and Karim did the same. The melody was soft and gentle. Nothing like the monstrous wails of the banshee

"What do you think is behind there?" Peter said.

"I'm hoping a way out of this lake …" Karim replied.

"What about that music though?" Peter questioned. "What if it's not a way out? What if … what if it's to keep the creatures of the lake outside."

"We won't know until we open it," Karim said.

"How are we going to do that? The key could be anywhere in the house." Peter sighed.

"We've got to try at least," Karim said but Peter seemed to be frozen to the spot. "I can't do this without you," Karim added gently

"Okay, come on then." Peter stepped out of the closet and Karim followed behind him, taking one last look at the secret doorway. The faint hum of the music continued to echo in his ears. "But let's cover the windows first. That banshee is creeping me out."

Karim and Peter ran up to the wizard's room, grabbed as many sheets as they possibly could and covered the windows of the house so that the banshee couldn't see what they were doing. When they ran out of sheets, they used the wizard's clothes. Next, they searched the house for the key to the latch, but the task proved impossible.

Frustrated, Karim took a fork from the kitchen, and tried to unlock the door with it, but he failed. Feeling his earlier determination waver, Karim threw the fork across the room and buried his face in his hands.

"What if the wizard took the key with him?" Peter said.

"He couldn't have. The wizard wasn't allowed to take anything with him," Karim mumbled.

"So, what do we do now?" Peter asked.

Karim unfurled himself and stared at the doorway, hoping that by some miracle it would open for them.

"I know!" Karim realised. "Maybe we can find a potion, or a spell that will help us unlock the door."

Peter smiled and they exchanged a triumphant look.

"I saw a library next to the wizard's room yesterday – we should check that out as well," Peter said as they made their way to the potion room.

An Unexpected Key

Ruffling through the pages of *The Perfect Guide to the Perfect Mix*, Karim struggled to find anything suitable. Until the very end of the book ...

"Aha!" he said and showed the recipe to Peter.

✤ A Potion to Get into Places You Shouldn't ✤

- Crush one rose petal and mix in with snail water.

- Add a pinch of dried beetle and stir well.

- When the liquid turns red, place one hand into the cauldron for five seconds and remove immediately.

- In your hand, you will find the object you desire to get into the places you shouldn't. Warning! Do not remove your hand before the five seconds are up, and do not exceed the allotted five seconds.

"Sounds simple enough ..." Peter said.

Karim and Peter followed the instructions in the book, their hands working in unison to blend the magical components together. When Peter opened the jar of crunchy beetles, his face turned the same shade as the banshee's. They quickly realised that each time they took something out of a jar or a vial, it was magically replenished.

"The wizard must have used a spell to keep the ingredients from running out," Peter said.

The room began to fill with the aroma of rose, and a hint of metal – like when Karim bit his tongue once, and the taste of blood was enough to make him gag. The potion bubbled and shimmered in the cauldron until it turned a ruby shade. Karim watched the flickering flames, hypnotised by the way they moved and danced in front of him.

"Who's going to put their hand in?" Peter asked.

They looked at each other hesitantly.

"Rock, paper, scissors?" Karim suggested.

"You're on!" Peter said.

They geared up, a competitive glint in their eyes.

"Ready?" Karim positioned himself in front of Peter.

"Ready." Peter nodded.

"Rock, paper, scissors, shoot!" they shouted at the same time.

Karim looked on as his rock became enveloped by Peter's paper.

"Woohoo!" Peter screamed with a triumphant grin on his face.

"I guess that means I'll be putting my hand in," Karim pouted.

"I'll count you down," Peter said, stirring the cauldron as it continued to bubble away. Once it had turned the perfect colour of red, Karim gingerly dipped one hand inside the warm mixture.

"Five ... four ... three ..." Peter started counting, but a loud bang at the window shook them both.

Peter jerked, and the cauldron tipped over. Karim pulled his hand away as the potion spilled on the wooden floor, seeping through the cracks. The sheet that they had draped over the window slid to the floor, revealing the banshee's face.

Karim and Peter screamed and dashed out of the room, slamming the door behind them.

"We have to figure out what to do about that banshee!" Peter wailed, one hand on his chest.

Karim's ears were still ringing from the sound the cauldron had made when it'd hit the floor.

"We could try and see if the wizard left –" Karim paused. "What is it? Why are you staring at me like that?"

"K-Karim, your hand!" Peter's eyes bulged out of his face.

When Karim followed Peter's gaze, he fell backwards in horror.

Instead of flesh and bone, Karim's hand resembled an intricately crafted key, complete with a handle and teeth that glowed softly.

"How long did you count for before the cauldron spilled over?" Karim asked, his voice barely a squeak.

"Three, maybe four seconds ..." Peter confessed.

"And how long did the instructions say to leave my hand in there for?"

"Five seconds ..." came Peter's reply.

Something had gone horribly wrong. Instead of producing a key, Karim had become the key!

"Peter, what have we done?" Karim's voice trembled.

"It'll be okay – we'll find a way to reverse it. I promise," Peter tried reassuring him.

"That's easy for you to say." Karim raised his voice to add, "You're not the one with a key for a hand!"

"It's not my fault that banshee was outside the window – we both moved," Peter said.

Karim knew it wasn't really Peter's fault, but there was no one else to shout at and with each passing second, Karim's fear deepened. He lifted his arm up and down, unable to shake off the worry that his hand would remain like this forever.

"Let's go back in and get the book – see if there's a potion to turn your hand back into–" Peter paused, "flesh."

They searched for the remedy, but none of the potions offered Karim a way to get his hand back.

"We can try the library. There must be lots more books in there to help us." Peter stood up but Karim stared at the key attached to his arm.

"Before we do that, I want to see if this key opens the lock to the secret door."

"But don't you want to reverse the spell first? We can make a new batch." Peter looked at him in surprise.

"I do want that, but I also want to find a way out of this house. Come on – it won't take long." Karim rushed down the stairs towards the closet and walked through the kelp curtain. The music was still playing, though the melody was no longer dreamy and calm – there was a sadness and urgency to the humming that made Karim shiver.

"Are you sure about this?" Peter said.

"Yes. Here goes nothing!" Karim approached the latch, and his key-shaped hand pulled him forwards towards the keyhole. The air shimmered and the door creaked open.

Next to him, Peter took a sharp intake of breath.

"It worked," Karim whispered and to his surprise, his key-shaped hand slowly transformed back into living flesh. Relief flooded Karim as his heart swelled with gratitude.

"The spell stops working on its own – that's why there were no reversal recipes," Karim said.

Peter looked at the door as sweat dripped down his forehead.

He wiped it away and pushed the door open to reveal a concealed passage that descended into darkness.

6
The Cage

The tunnel twisted and turned, a labyrinth of shadows and cobwebs. Karim and Peter crouched low, feeling their way through the damp cold. The longer they crawled through the tunnel, the louder the melodious hums became. After what felt like an eternity, the darkness gave way to a warm explosion of colours. Karim followed the light until he reached what appeared to be a barred door. When he looked through the bars, Karim was left breathless from the shock.

Peter let out a muffled cry.

Below them was a small room, boarded-up and shrouded in darkness, and in the centre of that room was an enormous cage, shimmering like a crystal prism. Inside the cage were merpeople of every colour and size. Karim counted seven in total, and every single one of them had a unique colour pattern – one the colour of seafoam, another coral-pink, a third forest-green. As the merpeople moved, their jewellery, made out of shells, knocked against each other.

Sensing a presence in the room, the merpeople looked straight up at Karim and Peter. Karim was about to scream as loudly as he possibly could, but something stopped him. Maybe it was the sorrowful look in their eyes, or the fact they were in a cage. Instead of fear seizing him, Karim felt sympathy for the merpeople. He was trapped too, just in a different kind of cage.

His cage was a house – the lost house of Lockwood Lake.

A mermaid with knee-length turquoise hair and a silver fin that sparkled when she moved wriggled across the cage to get a closer look at them. Since there was no water in the cage, the merpeople moved slowly, and painfully.

"Who are you?" the mermaid spoke to them, and though her voice was soothing, there was also a sharpness to it. Karim was so enchanted by these creatures that he couldn't bring himself to respond.

Peter cleared his throat.

"I-I'm Peter, and this is my friend Karim."

The mermaid did not say anything right away, looking to the other merpeople and then back up at Karim and Peter.

"Where is the wizard?" the mermaid said.

"He's gone," Karim managed to find his voice. "He left us here in the house. We're trapped."

All of a sudden, the merpeople began singing a haunting melody. The volume swelled. Unsure of what to do, Karim edged closer to Peter until the mermaid with turquoise hair raised one hand in the air. The cage fell into a silent hush.

"I'm Aura," the mermaid said. When she locked eyes with him, Karim saw they were icy blue, like the Antarctic Ocean.

"These are my friends: Ophelia, Saturn, Zain, Starseed, Ligurian and Thormead."

The merpeople in the cage looked up at them in silence. "Hang on – we'll try and come down," Karim said, rattling the bars on the door. It hardly budged.

"Help me kick this open," Karim said to Peter.

They kicked against the metal as hard as they could until the screws began to loosen.

"Keep going!" Karim yelled, and with a few final kicks the bars fell to the floor with a loud CLANG.

They had to jump to get down, but Karim landed on both his feet. Peter leapt down next. The merpeople kept a watchful eye on them as they approached the cage. Aura's eyes grew large as he moved closer.

"Don't come any nearer! Don't touch the cage!" Aura warned, but Peter's arms were already outstretched. When Peter touched the cage, an invisible force repelled him, throwing him backwards against the wall. He groaned as Karim rushed to his side.

"Peter, are you okay?" Karim helped him up to his feet.

Peter winced, his face twisting in pain.

"What was that?" Karim turned to the merpeople.

"A barrier the wizard put around the cage, to stop us from getting out," Aura explained.

"The wizard put you in this cage?" Karim asked.

"He and the banshee – they were working together."

"How do you mean?" Peter said.

The merpeople began a mournful song, singing in perfect harmony.

> "Once, we roamed the lake,
> Our voice a beautiful melody.
> But a wizard, desperate and cursed,
> Sought our magic to quench his thirst."

"How did the wizard trap you?" Peter asked.

"The banshee lured us into the house."

"Wait, are you telling us that the banshee can come into the wizard's house?"

Aura nodded.

"Yes – any lake creature can, but it still would not have broken the curse."

Karim felt a wave of terror. All this time, he'd thought they were relatively safe from the banshee, but now he realised how much danger they were actually in.

"Why was the banshee helping the wizard?" Karim asked.

"He promised the banshee that once he restored his magic, he would help find the rest of the banshee's family," Aura said.

"The wizard lied ..." Karim mumbled to himself. Did the banshee think that they had anything to do with it? Is that why it was always surrounding the house? Or was the banshee looking for the wizard?

"Why did the wizard think you would be able to help break the curse?" Peter said.

"At first, he thought by capturing one of us and putting us inside the house, he would be able to leave, but when he realised that wasn't the case, he got more and more desperate. He trapped merperson after merperson, thinking the more he had the better his chances."

"Why didn't he let you go when he figured out his plan wasn't going to work?" Karim asked.

"I don't know ... he came down here every few days with a book in his hand. I think he was planning something else for us ..." Aura said, and the merpeople behind her shuddered.

"How long did you say you've been in the cage for?"

"I don't remember," Aura said softly.

"We have to help them get out of this cage and back into the lake," Karim whispered to Peter.

"How do we do that when the wizard has put a protective barrier around the cage?" Peter dug his hands into his pockets and stared at the cage with a bewildered look on his face.

Karim turned to Aura.

"Do you know how we can get past this shield?" he asked.

She shook her head.

"We'll find a way to free you," Karim said.

The merpeople wriggled and hummed in response.

"Be careful," Aura said. "Do not open the front door under any circumstance – the banshee is a vengeful spirit."

With that warning in mind, Karim and Peter left the merpeople to climb up the hole and back along the tunnel. When they finally emerged out the other end, they were too shocked to say anything. Karim's mind was racing.

"Where did you say the library was?" Karim finally asked.

"Upstairs, next to the wizard's room."

"Let's start there," Karim said.

"But we have to find a way out of here too, before the banshee gets inside. Who knows what it will do to us then," Peter cried.

"I know, and we will, but we can't leave them in that cage, Peter. It's not right!"

Karim huffed as they climbed the stairs to the floor above. He understood Peter's frustration – he was frustrated too. He missed home. He missed Mum and Dad and Nan. He missed eating and drinking. That must be how the merpeople felt too, and they had to try to help them.

The Four Elements

In the wizard's library, Karim and Peter hoped to find a spell that would help them break the barrier the wizard had placed around the merpeople's cage. The heavy wooden door creaked open, revealing a room bathed in the soft glow of countless candles. The air was thick with the scent of aged parchment and sandalwood. Old, dusty books lined the corners of the room and there was a wooden table strewn with books in the middle.

"Let's split up," Karim suggested. "I'll search through the books on the table."

Peter walked towards the corner of the room. His eyes sparked with curiosity as he sat down to inspect the contents of these ancient texts.

Karim began by reading the titles of the books spread on the table, guessing the wizard must have been reading these books before they turned up at the house. He categorised them into two different piles. One pile for books about different creatures that lived in lakes and another pile for spells and charms.

Once he was done, he opened up a book titled *Enchanting Spells for the Weird and Wonderful*. The first page was blank. Confused, he flipped the page, but they were all blank.

"Hey, Peter, come and look at this."

Peter dragged himself away from the book in his hand and stood next to Karim. "What is it? Did you find something?"

"Not yet, but this is weird – this book has no words even though the title says it's a spell book."

Peter took the book from him and studied it carefully.

"Maybe it's invisible ink, and there is a secret incantation that we have to say so that we can see the spells," Peter said.

"But how do we find out what that incantation is?" Karim frowned.

Together, Karim and Peter scoured every page of the book until they found something strange spread across two pages in the middle. It was a drawing of the outline of two hands.

"What do you think it means?" Karim asked.

Peter was quiet. He poked at the page with his fingers, but nothing happened.

"I thought it might be a secret button to reveal the words ..." Peter sighed, but his words lit a bulb in Karim's mind.

"Give that to me for a second!" Karim felt a rush of blood going straight to his head. He laid the book flat on the floor, and carefully positioned his hands so they lay over the drawing. Not even a second had passed before the book wriggled under his weight. Karim kept his hands firmly in place, refusing to let go.

"Something is happening! I can feel it," Karim cried out just as the book snapped shut. He pulled his hands away just in time.

Peter's jaw dropped open so wide, it could have housed a bird's nest. Cautiously, Karim reached for the book again and opened it to the first page, which was now filled with words. All the pages were. They celebrated by jumping up and down on the spot.

"Let's see if we can find a spell that can break the barrier," Karim said. They paused when they came across a page that was emitting a bright beam of light onto their faces. Squinting through the white light, Peter read the spell out to Karim.

❧ ILLUMINATION! ☙

By the magical powers vested in me,
tap the thing you see,
a bright gleam will be revealed,
a glowing light will be unsealed.

"That must be how the wizard got all those lights in here!" Karim said, as the wizard's life down in the lake became clearer.

"I guess if the Council of Wizards stripped him of his personal magic, he still had these books to do magic with," Peter said.

"Exactly!" Karim said. "But he couldn't use any of it to get himself out. They must have made sure of that when they cursed him."

Spurred on by this discovery, Karim and Peter kept going, looking through the book for a spell that could aid them.

But their joy at discovering the not-so-secret spells plummeted when they realised nothing in the book could help them pass the barrier.

They spent nearly all day in the library, searching more books, and just as Karim began to lose hope that they would ever get the merpeople out, Peter squealed and jumped to his feet.

"I found something!" he shouted.

The air seemed to crackle with anticipation as Karim turned to Peter.

"Is it a spell?" Karim asked.

"Yes and no," Peter said. "It's a bit more complicated than just a normal spell."

"Let me have a look." Karim took the book from Peter.

It was titled *Spells for Sticky Situations*.

❧ A spell for passing through force fields ☙

Light a circle of candles and step inside the circle. Place four objects that represent earth, air, fire and water inside the circle. To contain the force field, you will need a crystal ball to absorb the excess energy. Chant the following incantation three times:

> Grant me passage through space and time,
> Hear these words, this cosmic rhyme.
> Ethereal forces, hear this call
> And let the protective veil now fall.
> Clear my path, and reveal the way,
> Grant me passage on this day.

"This is it," Karim cried out in excitement. Treating this mission like any other Adventurers United mission made things easier for him. Playing pretend felt lighter than accepting the scary fact that this was no daring game.

"Let's get the items and go back down there," Karim said.

They grabbed an empty bag from downstairs and placed a bunch of flaming candles from the library into the bag. The candles weren't actually lit by fire but by magic, so there was no heat from them and no risk they'd set the bag alight.

"The crystal ball is in the potion room," Peter said.

After they placed the crystal ball inside the bag, their search led them to a corner of the living room adorned with antique furniture.

Among the relics, Karim spotted a weathered stone, worn smooth by the hands of time. He picked it up and felt its solid weight in his palm.

"We can use this for the element of earth," he said.

"Yes, that will work," Peter replied, his keen eyes observing the room.

"This feather quill – can we use that to represent air?" Peter continued.

"I don't see why not, if it came from something that once flew in the sky," Karim said.

"There was a lantern in the telescope room. Let me grab that quickly." Peter ran up the stairs two at a time and a few minutes later returned with a red and gold lantern.

"Fire." Peter grinned.

"That only leaves water," Karim said, but ironically, that proved to be the hardest element to get hold of.

The taps, as Karim expected, did not work. Since there was no need for the wizard to drink, there was no water in the house.

"What about the vials of liquid in the potion room? We could use one of them for water?" Peter remarked.

"No, it has to be water, otherwise it might not work," Karim said.

They searched long and hard, but not a single drop of water was in the house.

"Peter ..." Karim said. "We'll have to open the door and take some water from outside."

Peter looked at him like he'd grown an extra head.

It was dangerous, Karim knew that, but what choice did they have?

"The merpeople said that the banshee can get in the house!" Peter paced up and down the kitchen.

"I'll do it," Karim offered. "You can keep an eye out for the banshee. All we need is a drop and then we'll have everything we need to save the merpeople. I'll use an empty vial to put the water in."

"Aren't you scared?" Peter asked.

"I am, but doing nothing is scarier, don't you think?" Karim said.

"Will the merpeople help us get out? Maybe they can swim to the surface and call for help when we free them."

"I hope so," Karim said.

"Okay, let me go and get an empty vial." Peter grimaced and walked away.

Karim clutched the glass vial in his hand. His heart was beating fast, and the glass kept slipping out of his hand because his palms were so sweaty.

"I'll do it if you want," Peter offered, but Karim shook his head.

"Let's get this over with," Karim said.

The water rippled when Karim opened the front door. It was dark, shadowy and haunting. Leaning forward, Karim scooped the water into the vial whilst Peter watched out for the banshee. Karim pulled the vial back and just before Peter went to close the door, a hand came out of the murky water.

Karim could feel sharp nails digging into his skin and saw bright luminescent eyes. The banshee was trying to get into the house!

"Help me!" Karim tried to untwist himself from the banshee's tight grip, but the banshee was too strong for him.

Peter put his weight behind the door, trying to block the banshee from coming into the house as Karim rolled the glass vial onto the floor so that it wouldn't break.

"The wizard isn't here! He's gone," Peter tried to explain to the banshee, but that only seemed to make it angrier.

"I'm going to step out into the lake," Karim told Peter.

Peter's eyes widened at that, but Karim had a plan. He took a deep breath and the moment he stepped out into the lake, he felt something slam into his chest. Karim kicked out as hard as he could, feeling the banshee's grip loosen as he was thrown back into the house. The door banged shut behind him.

He kept his eyes closed, afraid that if he opened them, the banshee would be staring down at him.

"It's okay – it's gone. Karim! Can you hear me?" Peter was crouching next to him.

"I-Is the vial here?"

Peter showed him the vial, with the water inside. They had the last element. Karim breathed a sigh of relief and lay back down on the floor.

Their plan had worked, just about.

The Number One Rule of Alchemy

Karim and Peter wiggled through the tunnel once more. The bag of items they needed to perform the spell was around Peter's shoulder, clicking and clacking as they headed towards the cage.

The merpeople stirred as soon as they saw Karim and Peter.

"We were worried; you have been away for a long time," Aura spoke and the other merpeople all nodded in agreement.

"Long story," Karim said.

Peter pulled the contents from the bag and started laying out the candles in a circle.

"What are you going to do with those?" Aura said.

"We're going to get you out of here – we found a spell that can break through this barrier," Karim told her.

The merpeople looked at each other in disbelief.

"Get inside here," Peter told Karim urgently.

In the circle, Karim and Peter laid out the lantern, the vial of water, the feather and the stone. They had the book too, so that they could recite the incantation as instructed.

"I'll hold the crystal ball," Peter said, clutching it tightly to his chest.

"Should we read the spell out together?" Karim asked.

"It might work better if we both say it," Peter agreed.

The merpeople dragged themselves to the other side of the cage, away from the circle of candles.

In clear voices, Karim and Peter began the incantation:

> Grant me passage through space and time,
> Hear these words, this cosmic rhyme.
> Ethereal forces, hear this call
> And let the protective veil now fall.
> Clear my path, and reveal the way,
> Grant me passage on this day.

They repeated it three times, their voices blending into one.

As the final words of the spell left their lips, the air crackled with energy, and for a moment, it seemed as though their plan had succeeded. The force field shimmered and wavered, offering a glimmer of freedom to the merpeople. Karim gawked as an arrow of light came towards them.

"Hold the crystal ball in the air," Karim shouted at Peter.

At first, the crystal ball seemed to absorb the force field wrapped around the cage, but before they could celebrate, the light grew in size. It seemed too much for the crystal ball to contain, and the glass shattered into hundreds of pieces. Karim and Peter shielded their eyes as a chaotic swirl of light zapped around the room. To Karim's horror, the force field was once again around the cage, which looked more secure than ever.

Aura had her head down when Karim approached her.

"I don't know what happened. We followed the instructions in the book – didn't we, Peter?" Karim said.

"Yes – it should have worked. I don't understand ... maybe we said the incantation too quickly?" Peter said, but it was pointless guessing what had gone wrong.

"It's the force field," Aura muttered. "We know magic, and whatever the wizard has done here can't be undone through a spell alone."

"What do you mean?" Karim said.

"I had hoped it wouldn't be the case, but there is too much magical energy surrounding the cage. Too much for that crystal ball you had. That's why it cracked."

Karim cleared his throat, exchanging a glance with Peter.

"We wanted to help. We wanted you to be free."

Aura turned her back to them as the merpeople once again broke out into a heart-breaking song.

"I'm sorry. We'll figure out another way," Karim said, though he wasn't sure where to even begin. It could take days, weeks, months or years. What about him? And Peter? What chance did they have of ever leaving this dreaded house?

That night, when an exhausted Peter fell asleep on the bed, yawning, Karim crept to the library and sat at the desk. He was tired, irritable and sad. The merpeople's mournful cries kept playing over in his mind, like someone had pressed the rewind button in his brain and it had glitched on a specific part of a song.

Absentmindedly, Karim shuffled the loose pieces of paper on the desk. Some of them he couldn't decipher – they were written in another language. Still angry at their failed attempt to free the merpeople, Karim threw everything on the floor. Papers scattered in the air; books went flying across the room. One of the sheets glued itself to his feet.

Annoyed, Karim peeled it off and was about to chuck it on the floor when he saw that it contained a diagram of the cage.

Karim was suddenly completely alert. He straightened his back and rubbed his eyes. He looked at the paper, and at the bottom, next to the cage, was a handwritten sentence:

> *Alchemy: humankind cannot gain anything without first giving something in return.*

Frowning, Karim read the words over and over again. What had the wizard meant by that? Assuming it was him who had written it. More importantly, why was it written next to a picture of the cage? Karim took the sheet and climbed back into bed, but he tossed and turned all night, thinking about those words. They appeared in his dreams, as a whispered song.

The answer came to Karim as soon as he opened his eyes.

"Peter! Peter! I think I know what we need to do."

Peter opened his eyes.

"The force field – we can try and get rid of it by offering something to it."

"What are you talking about?" a groggy Peter said.

"The spell we did yesterday seemed too simple, don't you think? If the wizard was powerful, he would have made sure the force field was well protected."

"I still don't get it," Peter said.

"Alchemy!" Karim said. "What if we offer ourselves to the cage in order to free the merpeople? If they go free, at least they can go up the lake and get us help."

"Let me get this straight: you want us to purposefully trap ourselves inside that cage?"

"I know how it sounds, but trust me, Peter. It's worth a shot."

"You really think it'll work?" Peter asked.

"There's a reason the wizard wrote this inscription next to the picture of the cage."

Shortly after, Karim and Peter stood outside the cage. They'd filled the merpeople in on their plan, and despite both of them hesitating, Karim knew they had to touch the cage. They had to test the alchemy rule.

"Ready?" Karim said to Peter.

"No," Peter said. "No one can ever be ready for this."

"We'll touch it at the same time," Karim said.

"Please, don't get hurt," Aura said.

Slowly, Karim touched the crackling force field, gripping onto the cage with all the determination he could muster. The room filled with lapping winds and shooting light.

Peter hugged the edge of the cage too, his hair going in all directions as the force field tried to push him away. They clung on, and Karim repeated the words he had read out loud. "*Humankind cannot gain anything without first giving something in return,*" he whispered over and over again.

Karim thought he was imagining it at first, but no – there was a calm filling the space around him. He shut his eyes, and he didn't open them again until the room fell totally still. Risking a peek, Karim saw that the merpeople were no longer trapped in the cage. Instead, they surrounded the boys, cheering and clapping. They flapped their tails and hummed.

"Where did the cage go?" a puzzled Karim asked.

It had vanished. The merpeople were free. Watching on in awe, Karim ran to Peter and they jumped up and down in relief.

"Thank you, from all of us," Aura said.

"But how?" Karim wanted to know why the cage had disappeared.

"A truly selfless act of sacrifice brings its own kind of magic," Aura said.

"How do we get you back in the water?" Peter asked, and the merpeople gave each other a knowing look.

"Now that we are free, you do not need to worry about us. It's our turn to help you and your friend," Aura said.

"Will you go up and get us help?" an excited Peter asked.

"Even better – you can go up there now," Aura said mysteriously.

"How?" Karim said. "The cage has gone, but not the curse, has it?"

"Now that the force field is no longer around the cage, we can use our siren magic to lift the house to the surface."

"You can do that?" Karim said.

Instead of answering him, Aura and the other merpeople began to sing. The house seemed to respond to their voice, shaking violently at first, and then Karim felt his stomach lurch as the house began to float upwards. He grabbed onto Peter to steady himself. The merpeople continued to sing as the sound of rippling water filled the house.

"Would you like to see the lake as we're going up?" Aura asked the boys.

"How? There are no windows here," Peter replied.

Aura took two shells from her hair and handed one to Peter and one to Karim.

"Press these against the wall."

Peter and Karim ran to the wall and did as they were told. Slowly, before their eyes, two windows appeared, revealing the depths of the lake. They could see fish of all sizes swimming in front of them as the house continued to rise. Karim had never seen anything so fantastical in his entire life.

As the house reached the surface, it began to move sideways, towards dry land.

"Here is where we leave you," Aura told Karim and Peter. "You can leave through the front door when the house lands where it once lay."

"Thank you," Karim said, "for helping us!" There was a crack in his voice, but only because he was bursting with happiness. Soon, he would see his mum and dad and his nan.

Aura took another shell from her hair. This one was different to the others; it glowed a bright golden orange.

"What does that do?" a curious Peter asked.

Aura pressed the shell against the wall, singing a song in a language that was both alluring and ancient. At least that was how it sounded to Karim and Peter. A small tunnel appeared in the wall, almost like a slide shooting down into the lake.

Karim and Peter helped the merpeople get down the makeshift slide and back into the water. Karim could hear them through the tunnel splashing, their laughter ringing in his ears.

"We will never forget your generosity!" Aura said, before sliding down herself.

Karim and Peter bid farewell. When Aura was out of sight, the hole in the wall shrunk, until it was completely sealed.

"Let's go and wait by the front door," an excited Peter said, so they headed back up and stood by the door until they heard a final loud thump. The house shook and then everything was still again. Karim could hear the chirping of birds, and the soft howl of the wind.

Gingerly, as if only just learning to walk, Peter took a step forward and opened the door, revealing the rolling green hills around Lockwood Lake. In the distance, Karim could make out his house, and he couldn't remember a time when he'd felt happier and more content. The bright light of the morning sun nearly blinded Karim as he stepped out onto the grass, but he refused to close his eyes.

"I'm hungry," Peter said, and they both laughed.

"Look, Peter, our stuff is gone," Karim noted.

"The wizard probably took it, hiding any trace we were near the lake." Peter shuddered.

"Let's go home," Karim said. "You can call your parents from my house."

"What are we going to tell them?"

"The truth," Karim replied, taking one last look at the lake.

Karim saw a figure by the window as they approached his front door, and before he even had a chance to reach for the handle, the door flew open. Mum and Dad were staring at the both of them, tears streaming down their cheeks.

"I knew I wasn't seeing things," Mum cried. "It's really them!" She wrapped Karim and Peter in her arms as Nan shuffled towards them.

The next day, Karim and Peter snuck their way back to Lockwood Lake, and the house. They wanted to see if all the vials and books were still there.

"This might be a waste of time – the police probably took everything," Peter pointed out.

"We should have got the stuff out before we told our parents!"

Peter nodded in agreement.

Peter was about to say something when he suddenly stopped walking, grabbed Karim's sleeve and hid behind the old oak tree just opposite the lake.

"What is it?" a startled Karim whispered.

"I think I saw the wizard!"

They poked their heads out from the tree at the same time, and just as Peter had said, the wizard was walking towards the lost house, though it was no longer lost. He had a spring to his step, whistling a cheerful tune. The wizard must have heard the news that his house was back.

"I can't believe he left us down there. We should tell the police that we saw him!" Karim said angrily.

"Let's go home," Peter whispered. "We don't know if the wizard has any of his magic back – he might try to curse us, or worse ... put us back in the lake!"

Karim wasn't listening. He was too angry at the wizard and had to say something. He ran from behind the tree and the sudden movement alerted the wizard, who spun round to face him.

There was a look of surprise in the wizard's eyes as he stood by the edge of the lake. His cheerful smile turned into a horrible smirk.

"Karim, get back!" Peter yelled behind him.

Karim opened his mouth to say something but saw a hand shoot out of the water, skeletal and green. Without warning, it grabbed the wizard and they both disappeared underneath the lake. Karim could hear the muffled cries for help from the wizard and a familiar screeching wail.

The banshee!

Karim and Peter turned to face each other, and it was their turn to smile.

"I think this has been our most exciting and dangerous mission yet!" Peter said.

"So where should we explore next?" Karim asked. Together they began to plot their next Adventurers United mission in the happy knowledge that the wizard had finally got a taste of his own medicine.

Now answer the questions ...

1 What was the first thing on Peter's list?

2 Why did Peter have his mouth open on page 20?

3 On page 27, it says 'The house would have been shrouded in darkness if it weren't for the bioluminescent plants that decorated the rooms.' What does 'bioluminescent' mean?

4 Why did Peter flick his hands away on page 34?

5 What did you think would happen when Karim put his hand in the cauldron?

6 What happened when Karim and Peter found the book with no words?

7 How did things change for the wizard by the end of the story?

8 Have you read any other books featuring merpeople, banshees or wizards?